Visual Overview Transduction from Physical Ene

Each of the sensory organs—eye, ear, nose, mouth, and skin—has a unique receptor for transforming a form of physical energy (e.g., light and sound waves, chemical molecules, pressure and temperature) into a neural code that is interpreted in specific areas within the cortex.

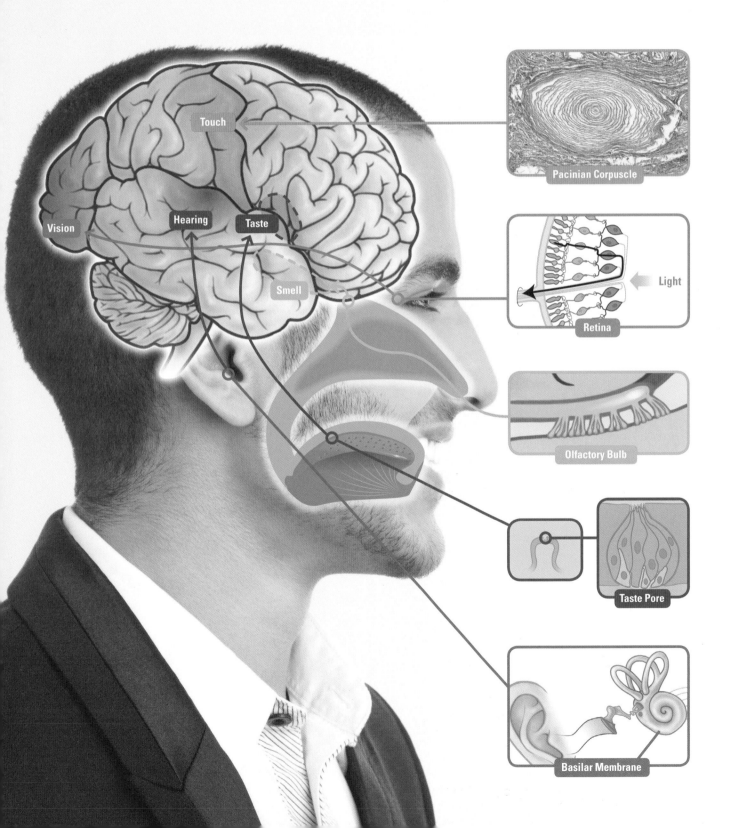

Touch

Vision

Hearing

Taste

Smell

Pacinian Corpuscle

Light

Retina

Olfactory Bulb

Taste Pore

Basilar Membrane